101

DRILLS TO IMPROVE YOUR GOLF GAME

Glenn Berggoetz
Alan Moyer

COACHES
CHOICE™

ISBN: 978-1-58518-257-2

Library of Congress Catalog Card Number: 00-105367

Cover design: Rebecca Gold

Cover photo: Jim Skinner

Interior photos: Courtesy of Christine "Bean" Berggoetz, Thomas "Flashbulb" Dwyer, and Jon Bricker

Text design: Jennifer Bokelmann

Coaches Choice
P.O. Box 1828
Monterey, CA 93942
www.coacheschoice.com

DEDICATION

To Bill Malcolm — For all the patience you had in teaching me, and for all the knowledge I gained from the time that I spent with you. Thanks, Bill. To my loving wife, Lauren, and beautiful daughter Allison.

Alan

To my mother, Rosemary Arnett — Thanks for everything, Mom. You're the best.

Glenn

ACKNOWLEDGMENTS

We would like to express thanks to the following people for their assistance with making this book a reality:

Brad Abbott; Dion Carver at The Club at Trophy Club; Tom Cleaver; Tim Dykstra and Travis Guisinger at Noble Hawk Golf Links; Mark Fowerbaugh; Gary Gant at the Pine Valley Country Club; Greg Griffith at the South Florida Golf Academy; Herm, Marge, Mike and Jan; Chad Hoyt; Denis Laymon; Mark Laymon; Doug Markle at Ridglea Country Club; Jeff McBride; Mephisto and Kevin; Trey Parker and Matt Stone; David Rohling; Springsteen and Thorogood; Kelly Mettert and Ron Vinson of Custom Golf of New Haven; and especially to Darla Pfenninger at GEM Literary Services.

CONTENTS

INTRODUCTION

The point of doing drills is to quickly train your body to get to the proper positions during the swing. Drills accomplish this by isolating one facet of the swing at a time so you can begin to feel where your body should be at all times. Sometimes you may only have to do a drill for a few minutes to develop that feel; other times it might take weeks. Just remember that building a swing is much like building a house: to make sure it's solid and stable, you must build it one brick at a time. These drills will go a long way towards helping you build that solid structure and helping you transform yourself from someone who merely golfs to someone who is a golfer.

We have broken down this book into 10 categories of drills, the first eight sections covering full-swing drills, and the last two groupings dealing with short-game drills. This breakdown should help you to quickly locate the drills you can practice to improve whatever aspect of your game on which you are currently working.

While many of the drills in this book are instructional exercises that we feel we have developed on our own and are unique to the lessons we give, many more of them are drills that have been around for decades. As a result, it is nearly impossible to be able to give credit to the originators of those drills. What we have sought with this book is to compile the best, most effective drills we know of, and by perpetuating the use of these drills, pay homage to all of the great teachers who have come before us.

One final note: When it comes to taking lessons, if at all possible, find an instructor who uses video equipment. At a minimum, this serves two purposes. First, the professional from whom you're getting the lesson will be able to pinpoint, in just one or two swings, *exactly* what you need help with—possibly saving hours of trial and error and guessing at what the naked eye often can't pick up. In the process, you'll save money and avoid frustration. Second, it will be so much easier for you to correct a flaw in your swing when you can actually see what you are doing wrong.

PART I:

FULL-SWING DRILLS

Drill 1: Address Position

PROBLEM: POOR ALIGNMENT

The easiest and quickest way to check to see that you are aligned properly is to set one club on the ground along your target line and another along your toe line. Ideally, the clubs will be parallel to each other, like railroad tracks. Next take a third club and hold it, first, along your thighs, and then along your shoulders. This club should run parallel to the other clubs at both spots. If all three clubs are parallel, alignment should no longer be a problem.

Drill 2: Address Position

PROBLEM: POOR ALIGNMENT

If you're having problems getting your body and clubface aligned properly to your target, try this. Align a 2 x 4 on the ground facing down your target line. Next, place a ball on the 2 x 4. Then place your clubhead behind the ball with the face squared to your target. Next, address the ball with your feet squared up to the 2 x 4; and take the time to visually note and remember how your properly squared-up body and clubface look now that they are in the proper position.

Drill 3: Backswing

PROBLEM: RIGHT LEG STIFFENS AT TOP OF BACKSWING, RESULTING IN A REVERSE WEIGHT SHIFT

Take your address position with both heels half an inch off the ground. Then, make a full swing, concentrating on keeping your heels off the ground and your weight on the balls of your feet. Stay on your toes throughout the swing and you'll maintain good balance; furthermore, it will be virtually impossible to stiffen your right leg.

Problem

Drill 4: Backswing

PROBLEM: EXCESSIVE LOWER-BODY MOVEMENT

If you're having problems with excessive lower-body movement, especially if your difficulties include collapsing your left leg on your backswing, try this drill. Place a beach ball between your knees. Next, take your normal swing, making sure to keep the beach ball comfortably in place. To do this, your lower body will have to remain more passive, thus helping to eliminate excessive, unnecessary movements.

Problem

Drill 5: Backswing

PROBLEM: RAISING UP ON BACKSWING

If you're having problems maintaining your spine angle because you raise up on your backswing, have someone hold the grip of a club out just above your head when you take your address position. Then, take a swing, focusing on keeping your head down while you feel your body rotating around your stabilized spine. If your head bumps into the club, you're still raising up and losing your spine angle.

Drill 6: Backswing

PROBLEM: POOR WRIST COCK

To develop a feel for getting in the proper position at the top of the backswing with a good wrist cock, try the following: Address the ball, and then, moving only your wrists, raise your club straight up towards your face, stopping when the club is one and a half to two feet from your face and at the same angle as your spine. From there, turn your back to your target and raise your arms—you're now in the proper position at the top of your backswing. Repeat this drill until the proper wrist cock and hand positioning feel comfortable.

Drill 7: Backswing

PROBLEM: TOO MUCH LATERAL MOVEMENT BACK

To teach yourself to keep from swaying too far to your right on your backswing, place a three-foot long dowel rod or club shaft in the ground outside of your right heel. Then, take your swing. If you bump into the dowel rod/club shaft on your backswing, you're letting your lower body sway too far to the right, rather than having your hips rotate around your lower spine.

Problem

Drill 8: Backswing

PROBLEM: RIGHT ELBOW FLIES OUT AT TOP OF BACKSWING

To remedy this problem, hit some balls using your right arm only. To maintain any semblance of control over the club at the top of your backswing, you'll have to have your elbow in the proper 90-degree angle position. Don't worry about hitting beautiful shots while doing this drill. Simply concentrate on getting in the proper position at the top of your swing.

Problem

Drill 9: Backswing

PROBLEM: RIGHT ELBOW FLIES OUT AT TOP OF BACKSWING

Place a beach ball between your elbows at address and hit some balls. If you keep your right elbow in the proper position at the top of your backswing, the beach ball will stay comfortably in place.

Problem

Drill 10: Backswing

PROBLEM: NOT COMPLETING BACKSWING/FOLLOW-THROUGH

If you find yourself cutting your backswing short and/or not completing your follow-through, put a swing weight on your club and take plenty of smooth, easy practice swings. Allow the extra weight to gently elongate your swing so you can feel what a full backswing and a complete follow-through feel like. Do this drill on a daily basis until this relaxed, full swing feels natural.

Drill 11: Backswing

PROBLEM: LOW SWING PLANE

To get a feel for developing a higher swing plane, set up over a ball in your finished follow-through position. Next, swing quickly in reverse (be sure to avoid making contact with the ball you've addressed), allowing the momentum and weight of the club to pull you back into a high, full backswing position. From this nice, high backswing position, proceed to the completion of your swing.

Problem

Drill 12: Backswing

PROBLEM: LOSING YOUR SPINE ANGLE ON BACKSWING

Use the inside of your elbows to hold a club behind your back. Then, take your address position and rotate your shoulders to the top of your backswing, making sure the end of the club points at the ball you've addressed. If the club points above the ball, you're raising up and losing your spine angle.

Drill 13: Swing Path

PROBLEM: CASTING THE CLUB

Holding the angle formed by your left arm and your club for as long as possible on the downswing is paramount in attaining crisp, solid contact with the ball on a consistent basis. If you're losing this angle early by casting the clubhead out away from your body with your right hand as you begin your downswing, try taking some full swings using only your right arm. If you cast the club while swinging with just your right arm, the clubhead will hit the ground well in back of the ball; hold the angle properly, and you'll make crisp contact.

Problem

Drill 14: Swing Path

PROBLEM: CASTING THE CLUB

Take your normal stance and normal grip, and then alter your grip in one small way. Take your right index finger and move it from underneath the club to the top side of the club where your thumb is. This action will form a claw grip with your right hand, which reduces the pressure of the right thumb and index finger on the club, making it nearly impossible to cast the club away from your body when you hit balls using this grip.

Drill 15: Swing Path

PROBLEM: CASTING THE CLUB

Take your normal address position, but use a cross-handed grip instead of your regular grip. Now, take some swings at three-quarters' speed and notice how this grip forces you to hold the angle formed by your left arm and the club, thereby keeping you from casting the club away from your body at the start of your downswing. This is a drill you can do either when hitting balls or while just taking some practice swings.

Drill 16: Swing Path

PROBLEM: CASTING THE CLUB

This is a drill you can do just about anywhere if you're having problems with casting the club out away from your body on your downswing. Simply turn your club over, grip it by the hosel, and swing. If you cast the club away from your body on the swing, you'll hear a swoosh sound before the club reaches the impact zone. If you drop the club in the slot and swing with an inside-to-inside swing path, you'll hear the swoosh sound as the club passes through the impact zone.

Problem

Drill 17: Swing Path

PROBLEM: POOR SWING PATH

To help yourself visualize and actualize a proper swing path through the impact zone, place three yards of ribbon on the ground along your target line. Then, tee a ball through the ribbon so approximately two yards of the ribbon extend out towards your target. Address the ball, then slowly rotate your head so you can look at the entire length of ribbon, and then swing. This will help you to visualize your swing path and target line, a process that will soon have you actualizing a better swing path. This drill will also help with your alignment.

Drill 18: Swing Path

PROBLEM: COMING OVER THE TOP

Without a club, take your address position approximately two feet away from a wall; then extend your left hand out until it's just touching the wall. Now, swing your right arm back on a full backswing and come through the impact zone without touching the wall. If you cast your right hand out away from you in an attempt to come over the top, your right hand will hit the wall. Drop your right elbow in the slot in order to take an inside swing path into the impact zone; as a result you'll never touch the wall.

Drill 19: Swing Path

PROBLEM: COMING OVER THE TOP

To get the feel of coming at the ball from an inside swing path, address the ball with your right foot placed behind your left foot. To make solid, consistent contact from this address position and to maintain proper balance, you'll have to attack the ball from an inside swing path.

Problem

Drill 20: Swing Path

PROBLEM: COMING OVER THE TOP

If you're coming over the top and entering the impact zone from an outside swing path, try this drill. At address, tell yourself the sole purpose of your next swing is to push the ball as far to the right as you can. Visualize yourself as a baseball player who is trying to line the ball into right field. To accomplish this, you'll have to attack the ball from an inside-swing path, making it impossible to come over the top. After you get to where you can consistently attack the ball from an inside path, modify the path so you are able to hit the ball straighter and not so far to the right.

Drill 21: Swing Path

PROBLEM: OUTSIDE-TO-INSIDE SWING PATH

One of the simplest ways to help develop that all-important inside-to-inside swing path is to address the ball, and then pull your right foot back about six inches. Now, hit the ball while swinging along your target line. To hit the ball anywhere close to your target, you'll have to swing inside-to-inside.

Drill 22: Swing Path

PROBLEM: CUTTING ACROSS THE BALL

Take your normal address position, and then split your hands two to three inches apart and take a full swing at three-quarters' speed. The split grip will force you to come at the ball from an inside-swing path if you're going to make solid contact with the ball.

Drill 23: Swing Path

PROBLEM: OUTSIDE-TO-INSIDE SWING PATH

Lay a 2 x 4 parallel to your target line and two inches to the outside of the ball you're about to hit. Make sure the 2 x 4 extends at least 18 inches behind and in front of the ball. Now, go ahead and take your swing without touching the 2 x 4. If you try to cut across the ball, your club will skip across the 2 x 4. If you have a really bad problem with cutting across the ball and are afraid of damaging a club if you do this drill, start with the 2 x 4 at least three or four inches to the outside of the ball you are going to hit. As your swing improves and you gain confidence with the drill, gradually move the 2 x 4 closer to the ball.

Drill 24: Weight Shift

PROBLEM: WEIGHT STAYS BACK AFTER IMPACT

Using an iron, take your address position over a teed-up ball. On your backswing, slide your left foot back so it touches your right foot when you reach the top of your backswing. As you begin your downswing, stride your left foot back to where it started, approaching the impact zone much as you would in a baseball swing. This added momentum should help you flow into a full weight shift after impact, thereby allowing your weight to finish over your left leg.

Drill 25: Weight Shift

PROBLEM: WEIGHT STAYS BACK AFTER IMPACT

Take your stance with your feet eight to ten inches apart. Now, take your normal swing, but make sure your right knee comes forward and touches your left knee on your follow-through, an action that will force your weight onto your left side.

Drill 26: Weight Shift

PROBLEM: WEIGHT STAYS BACK AFTER IMPACT

If you're not getting your weight on your left side after impact, hit some balls in which you take a step down the fairway with your right foot as soon after impact as possible. This will force your weight to come forward, and soon, a proper weight shift will feel natural and comfortable.

Drill 27: Weight Shift

PROBLEM: SWAYING

If you're having problems with excess body movement and with not swinging around your spine, try this: Grab your driver and tee a ball up high. Now, get down on your knees, address the ball, and hit it. Hitting from this position forces you to rotate around your spine and maintain good balance.

Drill 28: Weight Shift

PROBLEM: SWAYING

Take your normal address position, and then move your feet together until they are touching. Now, take a full, controlled swing, concentrating on maintaining good balance and rotating around your spine. If your body sways, you'll quickly lose your balance and be unable to make solid, if any, contact with the ball. Maintain your balance, and you'll be able to hit the ball as solidly as you do on your normal good shots.

Drill 29: Weight Shift

PROBLEM: SWAYING

Address a ball while standing on your right foot only. From this one-legged position, take a full, three-quarters speed swing, concentrating on rotating around your spine so you can maintain your balance. If you allow your body to sway, you'll quickly lose your balance and be unable to hit the ball well. Maintain your balance, and you'll be able to make solid contact.

Drill 30: Weight Shift

PROBLEM: POOR WEIGHT SHIFT

Find a place where you can hit from a slight uphill lie, which will force you to get your weight on your right side during your backswing. Then, immediately after impact, let go of the club with your right hand, which will force your weight onto your left side. Use a 10-finger grip while performing this drill to make it easier for you to release your right hand off the club after impact.

Drill 31: Weight Shift

PROBLEM: DIVING INTO THE BALL

If you're having problems keeping your weight back at impact, hit some balls where you keep your right heel on the ground after impact. This will keep you from diving forward into the ball and help you develop a feel for staying behind the ball at impact.

Drill 32: Weight Shift

PROBLEM: BODY GETTING OUT AHEAD OF ARMS

If your hands are dragging behind your body as the club starts to enter the impact zone, take some swings in which you stop at the top of your backswing for a two count, and then complete your swing. This will keep your body from rushing forward and allow for a more synchronized swing.

Problem

Drill 33: Weight Shift

PROBLEM: BODY GETTING OUT AHEAD OF ARMS

Without a club, take your normal stance with your left foot planted at the base of a wall. Place your left arm across your chest and take a half-speed full swing with your right arm, keeping your palms open. As your right hand enters the impact zone, it should gently slap into the wall without your left hip making contact with the wall. (Your hip should have rotated open.) If your hip contacts the wall before your hand does, it means your body is swaying, and your hands are powerlessly dragging behind. Do this drill until you can consistently have your right palm contact the wall before your hip does.

Improper

Drill 34: Weight Shift

PROBLEM: POOR BALANCE DUE TO SWINGING TOO HARD

If you're losing your balance during your swing due to the simple fact that you swing too hard, try this drill. Get out your oldest, most worn-out pair of sneakers, and wear them out to the practice range either just after it's rained or early in the morning when there's still plenty of dew on the ground. Now, start to hit balls. You will quickly find that an out-of-control swing will have you slipping all over the place, while a smooth, rhythmic swing won't be bothered at all by the moisture or the sneakers.

Drill 35: Impact Position

PROBLEM: NOT STAYING BEHIND THE BALL AT IMPACT

Using a wood with the ball teed up, address the ball with your left heel raised two inches off the ground. Keep your heel raised throughout the duration of your swing, which will force you to keep your weight back. After impact, let your right hand come off the club to allow your weight to come forward. Use a 10-finger grip to make your releasing of the club easier.

Drill 36: Impact Position

PROBLEM: NOT STAYING BEHIND THE BALL AT IMPACT

Using your driver, tee a ball up at least two to two and a half inches high. Now, hit the ball. You will quickly find that the only way to make solid contact with the ball teed up this high is to keep your weight behind the ball at impact.

Drill 37: Impact Position

PROBLEM: HEAD DIVES DOWN AT THE BALL AT IMPACT

Take your address position, and then have someone stand straight across from you, holding out a club so the grip is just below your chin. Now, take your swing, focusing on maintaining your spine angle throughout the swing. If you do a good job of maintaining your spine angle and keeping your head up, your chin will stay above the club.

Drill 38: Impact Position

PROBLEM: HITTING A LOT OF FAT SHOTS

Place a tee in the ground a quarter of an inch behind the ball you're about to hit, leaving just the very top of the tee sticking out of the ground. Now, hit the ball, focusing on using a descending blow in which the clubhead misses the tee and makes contact with the ball before touching the ground.

Drill 39: Impact Position

PROBLEM: POOR TIMING

If you're having problems getting your arms in sync with your body at impact, this drill should help. Address the ball and begin your backswing, stopping when your hands reach waist level. Your hands should be fully cocked at this point, (i.e., the shaft of your club should be pointing straight up). From here, begin your downswing, stopping your follow-through at waist level. Your club should be pointing straight up at this completed follow-through position. Don't worry about how far you hit the ball; just concentrate on making a synchronized, fluid swing.

Drill 40: Impact Position

PROBLEM: ARMS LAGGING BEHIND BODY AT IMPACT

If your body is getting out in front of your arms at impact, hit some balls using only your left arm. In order to make solid contact with the ball while using this kind of swing, you must keep your body behind the ball. Get your body out in front with your arm dragging behind, and you'll drive the clubhead into the ground.

Drill 41: Impact Position

PROBLEM: TOO MUCH LATERAL MOVEMENT FORWARD

To keep yourself from swaying too far forward as you reach the impact position, place a three-foot long dowel rod or club shaft in the ground just outside your left heel. Now, take your swing, concentrating on keeping your weight back and not letting your body bump into the dowel rod/club shaft until after you have made contact with the ball.

Drill 42: Impact Position

PROBLEM: BLOCKING SHOTS TO THE RIGHT

If your left elbow is separating from your side at impact and causing you to block shots to your right, place a clubhead cover in your left armpit before you swing. If you keep your left elbow against your body properly, the clubhead cover will stay in place until your hands are shoulder high in your follow-through.

Problem

Drill 43: Impact Position

PROBLEM: FLIPPING WRISTS AT THE BALL AT IMPACT

Take half a backswing (i.e., take your hands back to about waist high), hit the ball, and then stop your follow-through below waist level, keeping your hands in front of the clubhead at impact and for as long as possible after impact. Once you develop the feel of keeping your hands ahead of the clubhead, you can work on developing a proper release.

Problem

Drill 44: Impact Position

PROBLEM: NOT SQUARING CLUBFACE AT IMPACT

Take some smooth swings into an old car tire. You'll quickly be able to tell from the sound and the feel of each swing if you're contacting the tire with a squared-up clubface.

Drill 45: Impact Position

PROBLEM: NOT SQUARING CLUBFACE AT IMPACT

Start with your club at waist level in your backswing, making sure the toe of the club is pointing straight up. Now, swing through the impact zone so your club is waist high on your follow-through, making sure the toe is again pointing to the sky. Go back and forth in this manner without hitting any balls, in order to develop a feel for squaring the clubface in the impact zone.

Drill 46: Release

PROBLEM: NOT RELEASING HANDS AND FOREARMS

If you tend to block the ball, which leads either to pushing the ball to the right or to big slices, this drill should help you learn to fully release at and just after impact. Address the ball with your back and feet turned almost 90 degrees to the target so your back is facing towards your target. Your feet should be eight to 10 inches apart, and the ball should be teed up about half an inch. Using a mid-iron, hit balls to the target. You will find that you must excessively release your hands and forearms to hook the ball towards your target. After you get used to the feel of an excessive release, you can modify it into your normal swing.

Drill 47: Release

PROBLEM: POOR RELEASE

If you're blocking your release, take some swings with your right arm only. It's virtually impossible not to release your hand immediately after passing through the impact zone. Do this drill without hitting any balls until you can feel your hand releasing on every swing. After you develop that feel, hit a few balls while still using only your right arm, concentrating on maintaining the proper release you have just developed.

Drill 48: Release

PROBLEM: POOR RELEASE

To help develop a proper release in which your right forearm crosses over your left forearm just after impact, try this: Take your normal address position, and then split your hands two to three inches apart and take a full swing at three-quarters speed. You will notice that it is virtually impossible not to fully release the club just after impact when using this split-grip technique.

Drill 49: Release

PROBLEM: NOT RELEASING FULLY

This is a drill you can do almost anywhere because you don't need a ball, and you only need a small amount of room. Take your address position, but start with the club waist high on the backswing with the toe of the club pointing to the sky. Now, swing through the impact zone, but stop your follow-through at waist level, checking to see (1) that the toe of the club is again pointing up, (2) that your right forearm has crossed over on top of your left forearm, and (3) that the forearms are touching. If your forearms are touching, you've achieved a full release.

Drill 50: Release

PROBLEM: POOR WRIST COCK AND RELEASE

Address a teed-up ball while sitting on the front right corner of a chair with your right leg tucked back. Hit balls using a fairway wood, noticing that your wrists are forced to fully cock at the top of your backswing and that your hands and forearms have no choice but to release after impact. Hit balls in this manner until you develop the proper feel for cocking and releasing on every shot.

Drill 51: Release

PROBLEM: NOT RELEASING AFTER IMPACT

Take your address position, but hover the clubhead a foot and a half above the ground. Now, take your swing, but at the same time, imagine that instead of hitting a golf ball that is resting on the ground, you're hitting a baseball that's a foot and a half off the ground, and you're lining that baseball into center field. Feel your forearms release and roll over just after you pass through the impact zone in a smooth-flowing swing. As you continue to take these baseball swings, gradually hit lower and lower pitches, until you are eventually swinging at pitches that are on the ground.

Drill 52: Release

PROBLEM: NOT FULLY RELEASING

Using a pitching wedge, take your normal swing at a ball, with one exception. At impact, release your hands as quickly and fully as possible in an attempt to hit a snap hook. Because the club you're using is lofted, it will be quite difficult to get the ball to draw. When you get to the point where you can hit a draw with your pitching wedge, you'll know you're fully releasing.

Drill 53: Release

PROBLEM: LEFT ELBOW FLIES AWAY FROM BODY JUST AFTER IMPACT; POOR EXTENSION AFTER IMPACT

Take your address position with a beach ball the size of a soccer ball tucked between your elbows. Make a smooth, relaxed swing, concentrating on keeping the beach ball in place throughout the swing until you reach your full follow-through position with your hands over your left shoulder. To do this, you'll have to allow your left elbow to extend out towards your target in a proper follow-through motion.

Problem

Drill 54: Release

PROBLEM: IMPROPER EXTENSION AFTER IMPACT

If your left elbow is staying pinned to your side or flying up and out away from your body just after impact, try this drill. Address the ball in your normal manner, being sure to use a 10-finger grip. Then, take your normal swing (at three-quarters speed), except let go of the club with your right hand just after impact. This forces your left arm to release and extend straight out away from your body, while not allowing the left elbow to fly up and out away from your body.

Drill 55: Release

PROBLEM: NOT FULLY RELEASING HIPS

If you're having problems getting your hips all the way through on your follow-through, take some swings in which your sole goal is to have your knees come together on your follow-through so your thighs are touching all the way from your knees on up. If you get to this position, your hips have fully cleared and released. If you're having problems getting to the finished thighs-touching position, narrow your stance by two or three inches at your address until you feel comfortable doing the drill properly. After you feel comfortable, continue doing the drill, while gradually widening your stance back to your normal address position.

Drill 56: General

PROBLEM: HANDS COMING APART DURING SWING

Place a coin on top of your left thumb and under the pad of your right thumb. Now, take your normal swing. If your hands separate at any point during the swing, the coin will fall out. Keep your hands together properly, and the coin will stay in place.

Drill 57: General

PROBLEM: LACK OF DISTANCE

To build up hand, wrist, and forearm strength, do this drill. Hold a wedge by the grip in your right hand and extend your hand straight out at shoulder height. Rotate the club 180 degrees back and forth for 10 rotations, and then switch hands and repeat. Eventually, build up to two or three sets and also to longer, heavier clubs. The lower-arm strength you develop will help you explode through the impact zone and pick up extra distance.

Drill 58: General

PROBLEM: LACK OF CLUBHEAD SPEED

Turn a club over and grip it by the hosel. Now, take some swings in which you try to get a louder whooshing sound out of the club with each swing. This will acclimate your muscles to traveling at a faster rate, which will carry over to your regular swing.

Drill 59: General

PROBLEM: POOR BALL CONTROL

Stand far enough away from a large tree so you can just clear it with a 9-iron. Now, begin to hit 8- and 7-irons over the tree by moving the ball forward in your stance and by staying behind the ball. After you develop the feel for that shot, begin hitting shots under the branches of the tree by using various clubs and moving the ball back in your stance.

Drill 60: General

PROBLEM: POOR DISTANCE CONTROL WITH SHORT IRONS

Take your pitching wedge, and before you hit each shot, decide how far you will hit it, changing the distance you want to hit the ball with each swing by altering the length of your backswing. For instance, hit your first shot 105 yards, your second shot 80 yards, your third shot 115 yards, your fourth shot 70 yards, and so on. After you develop distance control with your wedge, do the drill with both your 9-iron and your 8-iron.

Drill 61: General

PROBLEM: POOR LONG-IRON PLAY

A major key to hitting solid, consistent long-iron shots is to keep your weight behind the ball at impact. To make sure you're doing this, hit some long-iron shots in which you tee the ball up one and a half to two inches high. With the ball teed up this high, you absolutely must keep your weight back and hit the ball with more of a sweeping motion.

Drill 62: General

PROBLEM: POOR RIGHT-ARM POSITIONING THROUGHOUT SWING

Take your address position, but instead of holding a club, hold a golf ball in your right hand. From this point, simply swing your right arm back and through and toss the ball underhanded across your body and down your target line. This is the exact motion your right arm should take during your swing.

Drill 63: General

PROBLEM: LACK OF FLUIDITY IN SWING

If you're struggling with a rigid swing, line up four balls six inches apart. Then, hit one ball after another without stopping, allowing your body to flow smoothly from one swing to the next.

Drill 64: General

PROBLEM: OUT-OF-CONTROL SLICE

Take your normal address position, except aim your body approximately 45 degrees to the right of your target. Now, take a much flatter swing than normal and release the club as quickly and forcefully as possible at impact in an attempt to hit the biggest snap hook you possibly can to try to get the ball drawing back towards your target. Once you develop the ability to hit snap hooks and get a feel for it, you can begin to modify your swing plane and release to hit subtle draws, or at least to straighten out your slice a bit.

Drill 65: General

PROBLEM: OUT-OF-CONTROL HOOK

Take your normal address position, except aim your body approximately 45 degrees to the left of your target. Then, take a swing in which you take the club back way to the outside of your target line to a high, full-backswing position. As you begin your downswing, cut across the ball on an outside-to-inside swing path, and hold your release as long as possible as you attempt to hit the biggest slice you possibly can. As you get the feel for being able to slice the ball, gradually modify your swing path back more to an inside-to-inside path and release the club somewhat after impact to produce a straighter shot.

Drill 66: General

PROBLEM: INCONSISTENCY ON THE COURSE

Improving consistency often has to do with improving concentration. In order to help improve your concentration, hit some balls at the practice range where, even though you're using the same club on each swing, you have to hit a different kind of shot with each swing. For instance, hit a low-cut shot with your first swing, a punch shot with your next swing, a high draw with your third shot, and so on. This will force you to concentrate on every swing.

Drill 67: General

PROBLEM: INCONSISTENCY ON THE COURSE

To improve your consistency on the course, play simulated holes on the practice range. For instance, tell yourself you're standing on the tee of a 410-yard hole, and then hit your drive. If you hit your drive 240 yards, that would leave you with a 170-yard approach shot. In this instance, take whatever club you normally use to hit 170 yards, and hit it. If you hit it well, move on to the next simulated hole. If you hit it poorly, take out whatever club you think you would need to put the ball on the green, and hit it. Continue in this manner for nine or 18 holes. This will get you used to hitting a different club on each shot and help you to be more consistent.

Drill 68: On the Course

PROBLEM: CONSTANTLY GETTING IN TROUBLE OFF THE TEE

If you're having trouble off the tee but think the only way to be able to score well is to hit booming drives, hit all of your tee shots for an entire round with the one club you can consistently hit 170–180 yards and keep in the fairway. You'll be surprised at how well you score, and you will learn that consistently accurate tee shots do more for your score than stubbornly trying to blast huge drives every time you reach the tee box.

Drill 69: On the Course

PROBLEM: INCONSISTENCY ON THE COURSE

If you want to add some consistency to your game and learn to keep the ball in play more often, play a worst-ball scramble with yourself in which you hit two balls off the tee. Play your second two shots from the spot of your poorer tee shot, and continue through the entire round in this manner, hitting all your shots from the point of your previous worst shot. This will force you to concentrate fully on every shot, which will improve your consistency.

Drill 70: On the Course

PROBLEM: NOT ENOUGH SHOTS IN THE BAG

Play a round in which you don't use any woods. This will force you to hit more mid- and long-irons, and it will also force you to hit shots you normally don't have to, such as drawing a 4-iron around a dogleg on an approach shot when you can normally blow your driver through the dogleg, leaving yourself a simple 8-iron into the green.

Drill 71: On the Course

PROBLEM: NOT ENOUGH SHOTS IN THE BAG

To help teach yourself to hit a variety of shots, don't take any even-numbered irons out on the course with you. Since this will leave you between clubs on a fair number of occasions during your round, you'll be forced to produce some shots you normally wouldn't hit. While this might cost you a stroke or two during the round, the new skills you develop will help you shave strokes off your score in the long run.

Drill 72: On the Course

PROBLEM: LACK OF CREATIVITY ON THE COURSE

Play a round in which you use only one club for the entire round. One-club golf will teach you to improvise on the course by hitting punch shots, knock-down approaches, cut shots, bump-and-run approaches, and other shots you might never consider hitting during a normal round. Varying the club you use for this drill from round to round will further enhance your creativity on the course. For instance, use a 4-iron for one round, and then a 7-iron for the next round.

Drill 73: On the Course

PROBLEM: LACK OF CREATIVITY ON THE COURSE

Play a round in which you allow one of your playing partners to tell you what kind of shot to hit and with what club on every non-putt stroke you take during the round. For instance, your partner can tell you that you have to hit a high fade with a 5-iron from just 125 yards off the green. Or you might be just a couple feet off the green with plenty of green to work with, and your partner might tell you that you have to hit a flop shot with a pitching wedge. No shot is off limits, whether it's a draw, a fade, a bump-and-run, or whatever.

Drill 74: On the Course

PROBLEM: LACK OF CONFIDENCE ON THE COURSE

Play a best-ball round, hitting two or three balls from each spot. The score you post at the end of the round will be indicative of the types of scores you're capable of shooting with a slight improvement in consistency and/or concentration.

Drill 75: On the Course

PROBLEM: NOT KNOWING YOUR GAME AS WELL AS YOU SHOULD

A major problem many golfers have is not properly assessing their strengths and weaknesses, especially when it comes to realizing how far they hit each club. Since most golfers tend to come up short of greens with their approach shots, play an entire round in which you hit one more club than you think you need to on every approach shot, and see if you've assessed your abilities properly.

Drill 76: On the Course

PROBLEM: YOU HAVE A GOOD SWING, BUT DON'T HIT MANY GREENS WITH YOUR APPROACH SHOTS

This on-course mental drill is designed to help you hit more greens in regulation and lower your scores. If you normally play a fade, aim all of your approach shots at the left side of the green, regardless of where the pin is. When you hit your normal fade, you'll end up either in the middle of the green or on the right side of the green. If you happen to hit it straight, you're still on the left edge of the green. As a result, no matter what shot you end up hitting, your next shot will be from the manicured short stuff instead of the rough. Conversely, if you normally play a draw, simply aim all of your approach shots for the right side of the green and let them draw to the middle of the green.

PART II:

SHORT-GAME DRILLS

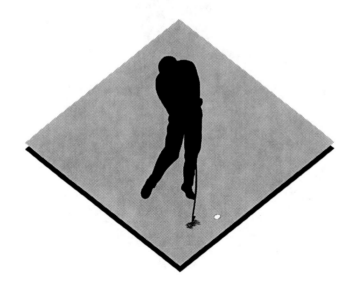

Drill 77: Around the Green

PROBLEM: INCONSISTENCY AROUND THE GREEN

To improve your touch and feel around the green, place three balls five inches apart, just off the green. Proceed to hit all three balls at the same target, but don't look up to see where you hit the balls until after you've hit all three of them; only then should you check your accuracy. This will help you develop a stroke for which you have a real feel.

Drill 78: Around the Green

PROBLEM: INCONSISTENCY AROUND THE GREEN

Tape or staple three paper plates at various heights onto a four-foot long dowel rod and insert the dowel rod into the ground, just off the edge of a practice green. Using everything from your 5-iron to your lob wedge and varying your distance from the plates, hit chip shots in which you alternately try to hit each of the three plates.

Drill 79: Around the Green

PROBLEM: POOR TOUCH AROUND THE GREEN

Take a bag of balls out to a practice green. Stand a few feet off the green, and begin rolling and lobbing balls underhanded towards a hole with your dominant hand. Roll some balls along the ground like a chip shot, and throw others in the air like a pitch shot. After you've thrown the entire bag of balls, gather them up, move to a different location off the green, and repeat the exercise. Take the time to throw hundreds of balls from various distances off the green to various holes on the green, concentrating on developing a feel for how you can best get the ball close to the hole and noticing what kind of trajectories work best for getting the ball close to the hole. This sense of feel will carry over to your sense of touch around the green with your clubs.

Drill 80: Around the Green

PROBLEM: NOT KEEPING YOUR HANDS AHEAD OF THE CLUBHEAD ON CHIP SHOTS

Stick a tee in the top of the grip on your club and hit some chip shots. If you're keeping your hands ahead of the clubhead properly, the tee will always be pointing to the left of your body, whether you're at address, in the middle of your backswing, or following through.

Drill 81: Around the Green

PROBLEM: SCOOPING CHIP SHOTS

To fix this problem, place your golf bag a foot and a half in front of the ball. To get the ball over the bag and heading towards your target, place most of your weight on your left foot, put the ball back in your stance, and hit down on the ball with a steep, descending blow with no follow-through. You might be surprised at how easily—and consistently—you get the ball over the bag. This should teach you to trust the lofting of your club to get the ball in the air.

Problem

Drill 82: Around the Green

PROBLEM: SHANKING CHIP SHOTS

If you're shanking your chip shots, there's a good chance it's because you're cutting across the ball and hitting it with the hosel of your club. To remedy this problem, lay a 2 x 4 half an inch from the toe of your club at address and parallel to your target line. This will force you to stop cutting across the ball on your swing and eliminate your shanks.

Drill 83: Around the Green

PROBLEM: POOR TOUCH ON CHIPS AND PUTTS

To improve your touch on and around the green, hit some putts and chips with your eyes closed. Use this technique: Address the ball, look at your target, look back at the ball, close your eyes, and swing. This will not only improve your touch, but it will improve your visual imagery as well.

Drill 84: Around the Green

PROBLEM: POOR TOUCH ON PITCH SHOTS

To help develop better touch on your pitch shots, establish targets that are 25, 40, and 55 yards away, and alternately hit shots to each of the various targets. To further improve your touch, perform this drill with everything from your 7-iron to your lob wedge.

Drill 85: Around the Green

PROBLEM: INCONSISTENT SAND PLAY

Draw a 10-foot long straight line in the sand and straddle the line, with the line being just to the left of the center of your stance. Move down the entire length of the line, making swings so your club contacts the sand at the line. After developing a consistent entry point with your swings, do the same thing again, only place a ball two to three inches to the left of the line before each swing.

Drill 86: Around the Green

PROBLEM: POOR SAND PLAY

Place a dollar bill in the sand and put a ball on George Washington's face. Now, take your swing, striving to enter the sand at the back of the dollar and exiting at the front of the dollar. This should help you visualize the proper path your clubhead should take through the sand when hitting out of a green-side bunker.

Drill 87: Around the Green

PROBLEM: INCONSISTENCY GETTING OUT OF GREEN-SIDE BUNKERS

To develop a visual image of what you need to do to get out of green-side bunkers, draw a six-inch square box in the sand and put a ball in the middle of it. Now, swing so your club enters the back of the box and travels in a shallow path through the front of the box, displacing the sand throughout the box.

Drill 88: Around the Green

PROBLEM: DIGGING TOO DEEP INTO THE SAND ON BUNKER SHOTS

Bury a 2 x 4 half an inch below the surface of the sand and place a ball on top of it. Now, hit the ball out of the sand. The buried 2 x 4 will keep you from digging too deep into the sand and teach you to splash the ball out of the sand and eliminate those heavy bunker shots that result in gallons of displaced sand, and the ball, invariably, remaining in the bunker.

Drill 89: Putting

PROBLEM: EYES NOT OVER BALL AT ADDRESS ON PUTTS

To make sure you have your eyes over the ball, which is imperative for getting a consistent read on your putts, address a putt as you normally would. Now, hold a ball between your eyes and let it drop. If it hits the ball you've addressed or the ground directly in back of it, you're where you need to be.

Drill 90: Putting

PROBLEM: LOOKING UP EARLY ON PUTTS

Stroke some four-foot putts, but instead of looking to see if the ball goes in the hole, keep your eyes focused on the point where your putter made contact with the ball, and listen for the sound of your ball falling in the cup.

Drill 91: Putting

PROBLEM: NOT CONSISTENTLY HITTING THE SWEET SPOT ON PUTTS

Tape two tees to the front of your putter, each tee one-half a ball's width to the side of the sweet spot, and stroke some putts. The tees will quickly force you to develop the ability to hit each putt on the sweet spot.

Drill 92: Putting

PROBLEM: JABBING AT THE BALL ON YOUR PUTTS

Address the ball, and then turn your attention to the hole. Keep your eyes focused on the hole and stroke your putt. Since this keeps you hole-focused and not ball-focused, you will hit through—not at—the ball.

Drill 93: Putting

PROBLEM: PULLING PUTTS

If you find yourself cutting across your putts and pulling them, place a 2 x 4 just outside the toe of your putter, then stroke some putts. The 2 x 4 will force you to keep the putterhead traveling along your target line rather than cutting across the target line.

Drill 94: Putting

PROBLEM: TROUBLE READING SIDEHILL PUTTS

Line up a 20-foot sidehill putt, and then place a ball every two feet along the line you think your 20-footer needs to travel to go in the hole. The last ball you place should be two feet from the hole. Now, stroke the two-footer in, and then begin to work your way back to your original 20-footer by stroking each ball over the spot where the ball in front of it had rested moments before. When you get back to your original 20-footer, stop and see where the previous nine balls have come to rest, decide if your line was good or bad, pick a line for your final putt, and stroke it.

Drill 95: Putting

PROBLEM: LEFT WRIST BREAKS DOWN ON IMPACT

Using your left hand only, line up an 18-inch putt. Without taking a backswing, sweep the ball with a firm wrist into the hole, finishing with your putterhead over the hole.

Drill 96: Putting

PROBLEM: WRISTS BREAK DOWN ON PUTTING STROKE

Putting with your left arm only, grip down the shaft of your putter so you're holding it just below the grip. Now, make some putting strokes, concentrating on keeping your wrist so solid that the grip of the club stays next to your forearm through the entire stroke.

Drill 97: Putting

PROBLEM: WRISTS BREAK DOWN ON PUTTING STROKE

Take some putts using only your right arm. This will give you a feel for what your right arm should do on the stroke. You will quickly find that the only way to make consistently good putts while using this technique is to keep your wrist solid throughout the entire swing.

Drill 98: Putting

PROBLEM: INCONSISTENCY ON SHORT PUTTS

If you find yourself missing more two- to four-footers than you care to, it might be because you don't have the proper visual images in your head of having seen yourself make enough of these putts. To remedy that, whenever you practice putting, use just one ball, and make sure you hole out that ball every time you putt. This means that if you miss a 20-footer by a foot and a half, don't just rake the ball away and try another 20-footer; instead, hole out that one-and-a-half-foot putt and then go on to your next putt. This will get you used to seeing yourself putting the ball in the hole and help you to develop the proper visual imagery and confidence to be an excellent putter.

Drill 99: Putting

PROBLEM: POOR PUTTING TOUCH

Place three balls three feet from a hole. Stroke the first one so it trickles into the hole. Hit the second ball so it hits the back of the cup before falling in. Finally, hit the third ball firmly enough that it hits the back of the cup, bounces up, and falls in.

Drill 100: Putting

PROBLEM: POOR TOUCH ON LONG PUTTS

Stroke putts of between 30 and 60 feet. But rather than hitting them towards a hole, putt to the fringe of the green instead, with your sole goal being to have your ball stop somewhere in the fringe. Direction is of no importance in this drill—you're only concerned with developing a feel for distance.

Drill 101: Putting

PROBLEM: POOR PUTTING TOUCH

Place 10 tees in a straight line on a practice green, with each tee being one yard apart from the one next to it. Now, begin stroking putts from just to the side of the line of tees, trying to get your first putt to stop between the first and second tees, your second putt between the second and third tees, and so on. After you've made your way out to the ninth and 10th tees, work your way back to the first and second tees.

ABOUT THE AUTHORS

PGA professional Alan Moyer is head pro at Willow Bend Country Club in Van Wert, Ohio. Alan uses the ASTAR Video Golf Learning System and has helped thousands of golfers nationwide improve their game.

Glenn Berggoetz is the teaching professional at JB's Indoor Golf in Fort Wayne, Indiana. Glenn uses the Pro Advantage Video System and has given lessons from Indiana to Texas to Arizona—anywhere his help is requested.